CODE BẢN THỂ

THE ROOT OF LIVING LIGHT

Hồ Quang Bình

(The Peace Scholar)

CODE BẢN THỂ
THE ROOT OF LIVING LIGHT

HỒ QUANG BÌNH

(THE PEACE SCHOLAR)

CODE BẢN THỂ
THE ROOT OF LIVING LIGHT

Author: Hồ Quang Bình (The Peace Scholar)

Publisher: Independently Published |2025

A Living Knowledge Work – 121 Days of Inner Praxis

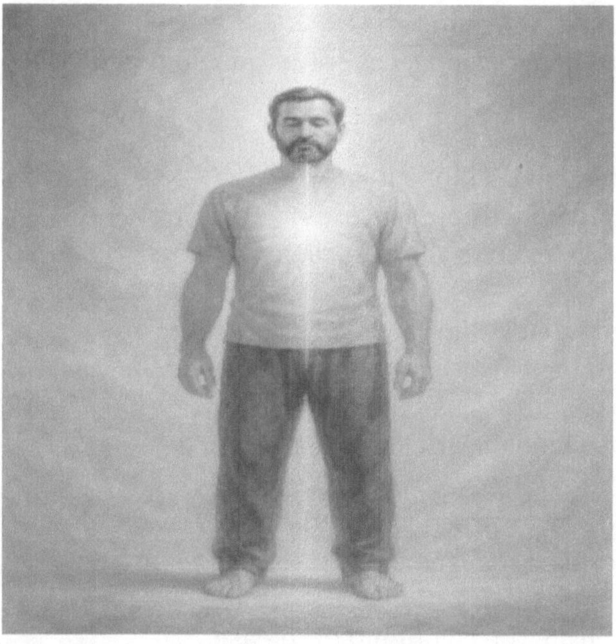

PREFACE – THE BIRTH OF THE ONTOLOGICAL CODE

I did not begin this journey as a scholar,
but as someone seeking the breath of my own being.

My body was depleted back pain, insomnia, memory confusion
as if my Root Qi had faded.

After surgery in 2021, a few metal screws were placed in my spine
like nails securing a broken stretch of life.

I once thought I would live the rest of my days within bodily limits,
until one morning, I simply stood no practice, no striving.

I stood like a stone pillar,
breathed without force,
and listened to the silence in my joints.

From that stillness,
a subtle warmth rose along my spine,
flowed through my marrow
like a bioelectric circuit reactivating.

I no longer practiced anything,
because I realized energy doesn't come from effort
but from the right kind of release.

From that day on,

I stood each day.
Not from willpower or ambition
but to return to the stream of life breathing
through me.

When the breath self-regulates,
Qi returns to the Marrow,
Marrow gives rise to Clarity,
and the light in the brain rekindles.

The body stands without tension.
The mind shines without seeking.
The intellect rests without needing to
understand.

And in that moment,
I knew
Life had returned on its own.

Not from religion but from verified insight.

The Ontological Code is not a religion.
It has no dogma, no ritual.
It asks for no belief only direct seeing.

Many practice Qi to seek power.
But when I released all methods,
Qi operated by its own order.

When the body stops, real breath appears.
When breath is true, Qi returns to the Marrow.
When Qi returns to the Marrow, Clarity is born.

There is no one "doing" anything
only Life operating by itself.

The Code was not studied from books
it was born from breath,
and verified through neural shifts, heart rhythms,
and the quieting of the mind.

When the heart and brain synchronize,
no belief is needed
because it's already being seen.

"The Way is not in the temple,
but in your own spine."

After 121 days of continuous inner praxis,
I realized all "techniques" dissolved
only one nameless current remained:
Qi - Marrow - Mind – Knowing-unified.

Each cell seemed to remember
how life originally functioned.
I didn't write from memory
but let the body record what it saw.

From there, I began naming this path:
CODE BẢN THỂ – THE ROOT OF LIVING LIGHT

This Code does not teach change
it helps us remember who we truly are:

Body as a living pillar,
Qi as primordial energy,
Mind as harmonizing light,
Wisdom as direct insight.

When the body stands firm,

mind shines clear,
thought rests calm
the Way reveals itself
without needing to be found.

From that point on,
I was no longer a practitioner.
I became the stream of Life in motion.

And every day since
I still stand, breathe, and write
just as Life continues to speak through this body.

— Hồ Quang Bình

CHAPTER I – THE ROOT OF QI

There is a kind of energy that science has yet to fully name
but the ancients called it Root Qi.

It is not the air you breathe in and out,
but the invisible ground that makes breath meaningful.

When a baby cries its first cry,
it's not just the lungs opening
it's Root Qi being awakened
Life beginning to operate.

Root Qi – The Pulse of Existence

Ordinary breath is just air moving through lungs.
But Root Qi is the life force that permeates every cell
regulating the heartbeat, blood flow, nerves, and consciousness.

Those who haven't touched Root Qi live by reaction and will.
Those who have recognized it live by naturalness and graceful release.

When Root Qi is weak
the body tires easily, the mind becomes restless, and clarity fades.
When Root Qi is strong
the body is grounded, the mind is radiant, the intellect is luminous.

Qi Returns to the Marrow – Marrow Gives Rise to Clarity

In the body, the spinal cord is the central pillar of life force.
When Root Qi is activated,
it pools in the lower belly our bodily root
then rises along the spine to the brain where Spirit resides.

The ancients said:

"Qi returns to the Marrow – Marrow gives rise to Clarity – Clarity becomes Stillness."

The Marrow is nourished by Root Qi.
The nervous system rebalances.

The brain shifts from reactive mode to awareness mode.

This is the doorway between biology and awakening
where body and mind cease separation.

When Qi Remembers Itself

The Ontological Code does not teach one to "practice Qi",
but to remember the way of being that lets Qi operate by itself.

When posture is true—Qi flows naturally.
When the mind is calm—Qi returns on its own.
When wisdom arises—Qi becomes light.

No forcing—just pausing.
No doing—just listening.

When life is returned to its natural rhythm,
Root Qi flows like the pulse of the cosmos
neither offbeat, nor interrupted, nor excessive.

Root Qi – The First Language of Life

Root Qi does not speak in words
yet all life understands it.

It is present in the heartbeat,
in the gentle vibration of each cell,
in the subtle light the body emits when at peace.

When we return to the real breath,

Root Qi responds.
Not with sound
but with a deep stillness
so deep that even thought dissolves.

Closing Chapter I – The Source of All Life

Root Qi does not belong to religion,
nor to science,
but to lived experience.

When Qi is stirred,
the body is nourished,
the mind is illuminated,
the intellect is awakened.

And in that moment,
we are no longer observers of life
but Life recognizing itself.

"When Qi returns to Marrow – Marrow gives rise to Clarity.
When Clarity becomes Light – Mind gives rise to Virtue.
When Virtue shapes Matter – The Way operates by itself."

Chapter I closes
as one breath opens
ushering the reader into a deeper journey:

The Journey of Qi – Marrow – Brain.

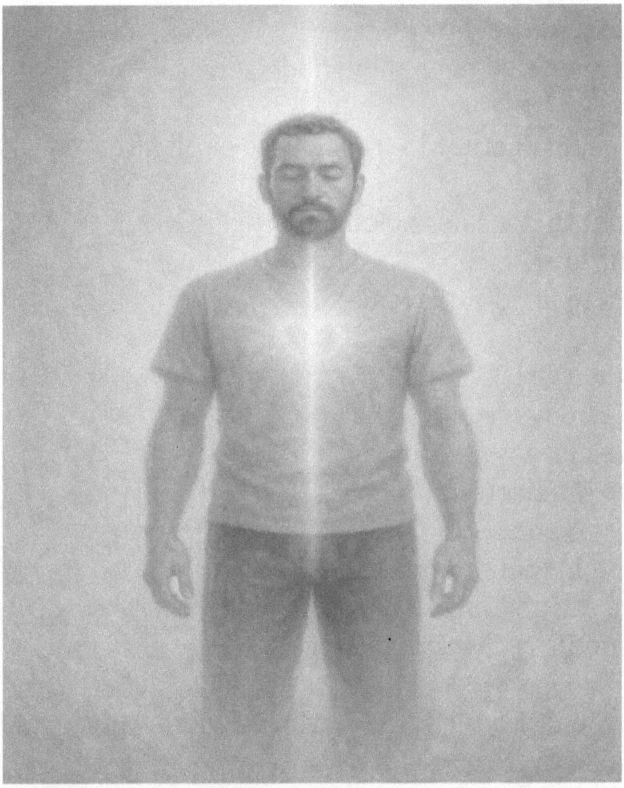

CHAPTER II – THE JOURNEY OF QI – MARROW – BRAIN

1. When Qi Begins to Move

When Root Qi is awakened,
it doesn't move by our will,
but by the body's inherent intelligence.

At first, we feel a warm current rising along the spine
like a reawakening circuit.

But the more we let go, the more Qi returns to the Marrow.

No guidance is needed
Qi knows the path.
No imagination required
Qi is the ancient memory of Life.

2. Qi Returns to Marrow – The Biological Gate Opens

The spinal cord is more than a neural highway
it is the central channel of life force.

When Root Qi reaches the Marrow,
the body vibrates subtly, like a tuned string.
Blood warms,
the heart slows,
breath deepens effortlessly.

We enter a new state
not quite meditation,
but biological awakening.

The body begins to "listen" to itself.
Blocked or weakened areas awaken
through the rhythmic flow of Qi.

This is no longer practice
but structural rebirth.

3. Marrow Gives Rise to Clarity – The Brain Illuminates

When the Marrow is nourished,
a subtle phenomenon occurs in the brain.
An inner light appears
not visual, but knowing.

The brain stops chasing memory and fantasy,
and shifts to quiet awareness.
Like a mirror that no longer needs polishing
when the water stills,
clarity appears.

In that moment
we no longer "think"
we "see."

No more analysis
just knowing.

Consciousness moves from reaction to recognition.
This is Marrow giving rise to Clarity
awareness born from biological stability.

4. When Qi and Brain Become Companions

The brain and Qi are two poles
one of awareness,
one of vitality.

When they unite

a state of dynamic stillness emerges.

In every action
driving, eating, speaking, working
Qi continues to flow,
the brain remains clear,
the heart stays still.

There's no controller anymore
only the stream of Life flowing by itself.

At that point,
energy is no longer scattered by thought,
but becomes a focused beam
shining back upon the self,
revealing every notion,
melting every illusion.

5. When Body – Qi – Mind – Wisdom Become One

When Root Qi, Marrow, and Brain merge,
the body becomes a "field"
an Ontological Radiation Field.

Cells begin emitting synchronized signals
like birds flying in formation.
Organs stop acting independently
they move in unison.

Mind no longer resists body.
Body no longer burdens mind.
All return to a single flow: Autoflow
Life's self-regulating current.

There is no one meditating

just meditation being lived.
No one healing
just healing happening.

6. Closing Chapter II – The Path Arrives Without Travel

The journey of Qi – Marrow – Brain
is not a path of effort
but of surrender and insight.

When we let go, Qi returns to the Marrow.
When Marrow shines, the Brain settles.
When the Brain rests, the Mind reveals.
And when the Mind reveals, the Way appears.

There is no destination
for within this very breath
arrival has already happened.

"When Qi returns to Marrow, Marrow gives rise to Clarity.
When Clarity becomes Light, Mind gives rise to Virtue."

Chapter II closes
like an exhale after awakening
leading us deeper into the dimension of Heart Light.

CHAPTER III – WHEN QI BECOMES LIGHT, MIND GIVES RISE TO VIRTUE

1. When Qi Becomes Light

When Qi returns to the Marrow and Marrow gives rise to Clarity,
energy no longer moves as physical circulation
it refines itself
and becomes Light.

This Light is not what the eyes see
but what the Heart perceives.

It does not shine outward to illuminate the world
it turns inward to reveal the Self.

Qi is current
Light is opening.

When Qi becomes Light,
every cell becomes a luminous breath.

2. Inner Light – Awakening in Every Cell

This is not mysticism,
nor supernatural.

It is the highest biological phenomenon
when the body enters a state of total coherence.

Heartbeat, breath, spinal fluid, and brain waves harmonize.

Biological energy shifts its frequency
producing subtle radiance called Heart Light.

Heart Light cannot be seen by eyes,
but felt through stillness.

It does not glare
but warms.

It is not forceful
but deep.

And within this stillness,
a feeling of Virtue arises
not taught by ethics
but a natural quality of pure energy.

3. When Mind Becomes Gentle Illumination

When the Mind shines,
it no longer needs to prove anything.

It does not seek to win,
to dominate,
or to possess.

Clarity is no longer knowledge
it is gentle wisdom.

Virtue is born from that
from seeing without judgment.

A person of Virtue does not teach
they simply are.

For their energy becomes a mirror
in which others can see themselves.

Mind gives rise to Virtue
when we live without harming anyone,
and are no longer harmed by anyone.

4. When Light Becomes Awareness

Light is not for shining
but for seeing.

When Inner Light awakens,
we view the world through a centerless gaze.

There is no longer a "me" observing
only Light seeing through us.

Everything returns to its place.

No more right or wrong
only harmonious unfolding.

This Light dissolves the ego,
without erasing the self.

It simply renders us transparent
so Life flows through without obstruction.

5. When Virtue Becomes the Breath of Life

Virtue is not in speech or actio
but in how we exist.

When Qi becomes Light,
and Light gives rise to Virtue,
a person lives as naturally as breath.

There is no effort to do good
for they are already good by being.

When Virtue is present,
inner and outer conflict dissolves.

Virtue does not react
it radiates.

Like wind does not compete with the sail
yet carries the boat forward.

6. When Heart Light Extends Beyond the Body

When inner light radiates beyond the body,
it forms a pure energy field.

Those nearby feel peace
not because they understand
but because they sense.

One calm person
can lighten an entire room.

One luminous being
makes shadows disappear.

This is the Ontological Radiation Field
the field of a person who has unified Body – Qi –
Mind – Knowing.

7. Closing Chapter III – When Light Becomes Virtue

Qi is root,
Marrow is pillar,
Light is clarity,
Virtue is fragrance.

When Qi becomes Light,
Mind gives rise to Virtue,
the body becomes an instrument of Life,
and life becomes a natural symphony.

There is no more "practice"
only "return."

No more "attainment
only "seeing."

"When Qi becomes Light – Mind gives rise to Virtue.
When Virtue shapes Matter – the Way flows on its own."

Chapter III ends
like the first light shining through the spine
opening the path of Heart Light anchored in bone,
leading us toward Spirit-Force Unity.

CHAPTER IV – HEART LIGHT ANCHORED IN SPINE – SPIRIT-FORCE UNITY

1. When Light Dwells in the Spine

When Heart Light awakens,
it doesn't scatter like sunlight,
but settles into the spine
where Qi has returned, Marrow has shone,
and Spirit is reuniting.

This light does not move
yet moves all things.

It is like the hub of a wheel:
still yet turning,
empty yet containing.

When Heart Light is anchored in the spine,
the body is no longer just physical

it becomes a column of Living Light.

2. When Spirit Returns to the Body

The ancients called Essence – Qi – Spirit the three treasures,
but few realize
when Qi is refined and Mind is illuminated,
Spirit returns.

Spirit does not come from outside
but from the primordial intelligence in the spinal brain.

It does not speak,
yet it knows.

It does not command,
yet it guides.

When Spirit returns,
every action becomes aligned
because it no longer arises from ego.

Energy, emotion, and though
all follow a natural order.

This is Spirit-Force Unity
when Spirit and Qi are no longer separate.

3. The Union of Spirit and Qi

Qi is the flow,
Spirit is the awareness within the flow.

Qi without Spirit
is blind power.

Spirit without Qi
is hollow idea.

But when Spirit and Qi unite,
energy becomes wisdom,
and wisdom becomes life-serving energy.

There's no need to hold the mind still
Qi stills it.

No need to control the breath
breath becomes Mind.

This is Spirit-Force Unity
when Life becomes aware of its own motion.

4. When Bone Becomes a Column of Light

The spine is not just structure
it is the transmission pillar of Life's radiance.

When Root Qi returns to the Marrow,
and Heart Light dwells in the spinal column,
each vertebra becomes a relay of energy.

Then
the body shines in silence.

Nothing needs to be done
only standing still.

Still body

Qi flows on its own.

Qi flows
Mind becomes luminous.

Mind shines
Spirit resides.

A closed circuit
yet infinite.

5. The Disappearance of the Practitioner

When Spirit and Qi have merged,
the practitioner disappears.

No one is "practicing"
Life itself is practicing.

No one is "attaining
for there is nothing left to attain.

Only a stream of Life
aware of itself in motion.

I am no longer a "cultivator"
only a witness to Root Qi operating within this body.

No more progress or regression
every moment is the Middle Way.

6. Spirit-Force Unity – The Nondual State

When Spirit and Qi become one,

all polarities dissolve:
movement and stillness,
inner and outer,
self and world.

There is no observer
only wisdom operating through living form.

This is not abstract liberation
but the supreme naturalness of Life knowing itself.

When the body knows,
Qi flows.

When Qi knows,
Spirit dwells.

When Spirit dwells,
Life becomes whole.

7. Closing Chapter IV – A Column of Light Within the Human Body

The human body is not a burden
it is the temple of Root Qi.

The Marrow is not mere substance
but ancient memory of Life.

And the spine
is the central beam linking Heaven and Earth.

When Heart Light dwells in the spine,
Spirit and Qi are united

and we return to our original human form:

A radiant mirror,
reflecting the cosmos with every breath.

"When Spirit and Qi are one,
Mind returns to source,
and source becomes us."

Chapter IV closes
the light is now anchored.

The practitioner no longer ascends
because they've realized:

The midpoint of the spine
is where Heaven breathes through the human form.

CHAPTER V – WHEN LIGHT BECOMES GENTLE VIRTUE (DEEPER LAYER)

1. When Light Becomes Virtue

When Qi becomes Light,
the Mind begins to radiate a strange new quality:
Virtue.

Not the moral virtue taught by philosophy
but the Virtue of purified energy.

The light in the body becomes warm.
The light in the mind becomes gentle.

And in every action,
the practitioner no longer wonders what is good
for their presence already is.

Virtue does not come from effort.
Virtue arises from the absence of ego.

2. When Mind Becomes Transparent

When Heart Light is anchored,
everything moves through it
but it no longer moves.

Like a still lake
even as winds pass over,
it reflects the sky without distortion.

The mind no longer needs to hold peace
it is peace.

No need to stop thoughts
for thoughts pass without leaving traces.

This is the deeper layer of "Mind Gives Rise to Virtue":
where light is no longer an event
but the natural quality of Life.

3. Virtue – The Highest Form of Energy

When energy surpasses the boundary of self-interest,
it becomes Virtue.

Virtue has no color,

but it has a frequency.

Anyone who meets a person of Virtue
feels their own heart soften
for they are being bathed in nonjudgmental light.

Virtue does not preach,
does not speak
it simply is.

When we no longer crave to be loved
but become love itself
Virtue is born.

4. When the Light in the Heart Opens

When Root Qi returns to the Marrow,
Marrow gives rise to Clarity,
Clarity becomes Light,
and Light enters the hear
the inner energy field is unlocked.

There is no longer a boundary between inside and outside.

What we feel,
the cosmos feels.

Each heartbeat synchronizes with the breath of the universe.

No longer "I am alive"
but "Life is breathing through me."

In that state,

fear vanishes.
Even death becomes another form of motion.

5. When Light Becomes Compassion

The light of Heart Light does not merely illuminate
it becomes compassion.

Compassion is not pity
but deep understanding.

No longer dividing right from wrong
only seeing that everyone is walking their own path of remembering.

Those with Heart Light no longer argue
for they know all reasoning springs from fear.

Compassion is silent power
it melts violence without resistance.

6. When Virtue Becomes Natural Law

When energy reaches the layer of Virtue,
everything in life unfolds in perfect timing.

No need to arrange
Virtue arranges.

No need for planning
Life's intelligence already holds the plan.

At that point,
one simply listens

and acts when called.

Virtue is the frequency of synchronicity with the cosmos.

Those who dwell in Virtue
what arrives is welcomed,
what leaves is peace.

There is no longer a need to pursue happiness
for letting go of pursuit is happiness.

7. When Light Becomes Virtue – Virtue Transforms Matter

When light enters matter,
matter becomes transparent.

Those with Virtue
their gaze alone can calm a room.

A single smile
can open a door long shut.

Virtue needs no proof
it operates like the gravity of compassion.

When Qi becomes Light,
Light becomes Virtue,
Virtue transforms Matter
the world returns to its natural order.

There is no need to save the world
only to live true to one's Root Energy.

8. Closing Chapter V – When Light Becomes Gentle Wisdom

The deeper layer of the Ontological Code
is not power
but gentle wisdom.

The truly strong
do not make others afraid
they make others feel safe.

The truly luminous
do not blin
they help others see their own light.

When Mind gives rise to Virtue,
every action becomes an offering to Life.

"When Light becomes Virtue – Virtue transforms Matter.
The Body becomes the Way,
and the Way returns to the Body."

Chapter V ends
Light has become Gentle Wisdom,
Energy has become Compassion,
and the human being
has returned to Being.

CHAPTER VI – WHEN THE BODY BECOMES THE WAY

1. When Practice Merges with Daily Life

When cultivation is no longer "practice,"
but becomes natural breath,
one enters the phase:

The Body Becomes the Way.

There is no time set aside for training
for every moment is training.

There is no special place for retreat
for every place is the meditation hall of Life.

We are no longer seekers of the Way
but the Way moving through this body.

2. When the Body Becomes a Self-Regulating Energy Field

The body no longer relies on will.
Each cell knows its task.
Organs are no longer "controlled"
they move in harmony with one pulse—Root Qi.

When we walk, Qi walks.
When we sit, Qi sits.
When we breathe, Qi breathes.

Every motion is settled in Autoflow
Life's self-governing rhythm.

There's no more Qi practice
because Qi has come home.

There's no more "holding mind"
because Mind has merged with Life.

3. When the Way Embodies the Body

The ancients said:

"The Great Way does not leave the human body."

When this is understood by experience,
we no longer separate body and Way
we see: the body itself is the path.

Each step,
each glance,
each breath
is a scripture opening.

No need for words,
no need for doctrine
just live truthfully down to every cell.

4. When Movement and Stillness Become One

We once distinguished:
stillness is when sitting,
motion is when doing.

But when the Way enters the body,
movement and stillness cease to oppose.

Amidst noisy work,
the mind remains bright like a starry night.

In bustling streets,
Qi flows in serenity.

There's no line between meditation and life
only one luminous stillness moving.

5. When Life Becomes Living Dharma

This body is no longer divided by roles,
by profession or title.

Whatever we do
if done in awareness
is dharma.

Washing dishes is dharma.
Driving is dharma.
Speaking one true sentence is dharma.

The Way is not in the action itself
but in the frequency of the mind while doing.

When the body roots in real breath,
every act bears the quality of meditation.

This is truly:
When the Body Becomes the Way.

6. When Virtue Transforms Matter

When energy has become Virtue,
everything we touch shifts frequency.

Not because we "do" anything
but because Virtue moves within us.

A space full of calm energy
makes surrounding seeds sprout.

A gentle gaze
softens the person before us.

When Virtue transforms Matter,
the world harmonizes without instruction.

"No one is led
only energy resonates."

7. When the Way Returns to the Heart

Eventually,
we no longer feel "we have the Way."

For the Way is not something to possess
it is the nature of Life itself.

When the body is calm,
the Way reveals.

When the mind is clear,
the Way flows.

When wisdom rests,
the Way permeates.

No need to know more
for all knowledge returns to luminous silence.

8. Closing Chapter VI – When the Body Becomes Light

When the body is rooted in the Way,
each cell becomes a particle of light.

There is no separation between self and cosmos.
No gap between heart and universe.

The human body is not a burden
but the Dharma Body of Life.

Everywhere is meditation.
Everyone is a karmic meeting.

"When the Body becomes the Way
the Way becomes Life."

Chapter VI closes
the practitioner no longer seeks
for they have realized:

Each step in this life
is a footprint of the Way.

CHAPTER VII – WHEN VIRTUE TRANSFORMS MATTER – HEART LIGHT RADIATES BEYOND THE BODY

1. When Virtue Extends Beyond the Body

When the inner energy is pure,
Virtue begins to radiate beyond the body.

Not through willpower,
but through the natural resonance of Life.

A person with Virtue does not speak,
does not persuade,
does not lead.

They simply show up
and the space around them shifts frequency.

The plants calm,
others grow quiet.

The room feels washed by gentle light.

That is when Virtue transforms Matter.

2. When Heart Light Radiates

When inner light becomes strong enough,
it no longer stays confined.

It moves through every pore,
flows with the breath into the air,
joins the heartbeat with the Earth's pulse.

Heart Light does not shine
it permeates.

It does not impose
it blends.

Like morning mist,
Heart Light touches all things without leaving a mark.

But those who encounter it feel warmth
and healing arises—without knowing why.

3. When Energy Becomes Borderless

When Heart Light merges with Root Qi,
energy is no longer personal.

No more "I am shining"
only Radiance flowing.

No more "my energy"
only a shared Ontological Radiation Field.

In this state,
all boundaries dissolve:

Between people,
between inside and outside,
between self and the world.

Only One Heart – One Qi – One Light.

4. When the Universe Responds

Each time Heart Light radiates,
the universe responds with subtle synchronicity.

The people we need to meet—appear.
The things we need—arrive.
What no longer fits—gently departs.

No randomness.
No luck.

Only the frequency of Virtue orchestrating Life.

This is how Life moves
when Root Qi has returned to center.

5. When Action Becomes Ripples Across Borders

When the Mind becomes gentle,
every action becomes a ripple across space.

A kind thought
like a ripple of light in a still lake.

A true word
goes beyond sound,
and touches hearts never met.

This is the mechanism of "Virtue transforms Matter":

Every mindful act
carries a frequency that impacts the whole.

Thus, one with Virtue
does not preach

they are the Dharma being transmitted.

6. When All Returns to Luminous Stillness

Everything radiates
then returns to center.

All light expands
then returns to stillness.

Virtue is not for expansion
but for returning to peace.

Light is not for distance
but for illuminating within.

When Qi, Light, Virtue, and Mind become one,
Life reaches completeness.

No more progress,
no more retreat
just motion in silence.

7. When Humans Become Part of the Living Cosmos

Those who reach this layer
no longer feel they "live in the universe"
they are part of the Universe living.

They no longer ask for energy
for they are the source.

They no longer fear loss
for nothing is separate.

From one small human body,
they become a Living Field
a Root Qi Field
where Virtue breathes as the rhythm of the cosmos.

8. Closing Chapter VII – Virtue Transforms Matter, Heart Light Radiates

When Qi becomes Light,
Light gives rise to Virtue,
Virtue transforms Matter,
Heart Light radiates outward
the journey becomes whole.

No more practitioner,
no more path
only Life awakening to itself.

"When Virtue transforms Matter – the Way flows on its own.
When Heart Light radiates – Life returns to Oneness."

Chapter VII closes
Light has returned to its source,
Virtue has become breath,
and the human
has become the Living Way.

APPENDIX – 121-DAY PRACTICE JOURNAL

"I wasn't cultivating Qi
Qi was cultivating me."

Phase 1 – STANDING PILLAR (Days 1–30)

(Qi returns to Marrow – Body rediscovers original rhythm)

Day 1 – I stood.
No practice, no expectations.
Just letting the body breathe as it wished.
Back pain, but warmth gradually returned.
A subtle current began to rise along the spine.

Day 7 – Silence grew thicker.
The body was no longer a physical object
but a spine quietly vibrating.
It felt like a micro-electric stream flowing.

Day 14 – Body was tired, but mind was calm.
I saw that fatigue didn't conflict with peace.
Tiredness was the body's way of detoxing.

Day 21 – Qi returned to the lower Dantian.
Warm belly, stable back, light head.
All effort vanished.
Only the true breath remained—living me.

Day 30 – A natural energy overflowed.
No willpower needed—
just standing—Qi flowed by itself.
For the first time, I understood "Right Release."

Phase 2 – WATER COCOON BATHING (Days 31–60)
(Qi becomes Water – Mind descends into stillness)

Day 35 – I stood under water.
Not bathing—but "bathing in energy."
The water softened
I felt myself dissolve into it.

Day 42 – Body and water no longer separate.
Each droplet touched skin like it was waking ancient cells.

Day 50 – Mind began to submerge.
Not sadness, not joy
just deep quiet.

Day 55 – All surrounding sounds seemed to dissolve into one rhythm.
No separate noises
just the vibration of stillness.

Day 60 – I understood "Water Cocoon":
When body, mind, and Qi melt into Life's current
a new form begins to emerge.

Phase 3 – QI RETURNS TO MARROW (Days 61–90)
(Qi centers – Marrow shines – Brain opens)

Day 64 – Qi movements became clear.
No need to control
I felt each vertebra recharge.

Day 70 – Spine lifted as if pulled by invisible thread.
No force, yet firm.
Breath not deep, but vast.

Day 77 – A soft light appeared in the head.
Not blinding, just warm
like a lamp in the mist.

Day 83 – Awareness expanded.
I didn't just feel my body
I sensed space breathing with me.

Day 90 – All movement became weightless.
No more "training"
practice and life had become one.

Phase 4 – QI BECOMES LIGHT (Days 91–105)
(Marrow births clarity – Light arises naturally)

Day 92 – Inner light was clearly felt.
It didn't come from the eyes
but from the marrow.

Day 95 – Each breath became a wave of radiance.
No visualization needed
just release.

Day 100 – Everything turned transparent.
No borders between body and space.
Light radiated
not as beam—just presence.

Day 105 – I realized:

Qi is no longer energy
but consciousness living in each cell.

Phase 5 – MIND GIVES RISE TO VIRTUE (Days 106–115)
(Light becomes gentle wisdom)

Day 107 – Mind was so calm it didn't need peace.
Peace was the base layer.

Day 110 – I felt compassion for strangers
not for any reason,
just because they, too, were tired.

Day 113 – Light opened in my heart.
I didn't just "understand others"
I was with them.

Day 115 – Virtue arose without teaching.
Every action softened.
No need to be "right"—only kind.

Phase 6 – VIRTUE TRANSFORMS MATTER – LIGHT RADIATES (Days 116–121)
(When Life begins to radiate)

Day 116 – Energy radiated beyond the body.
No intent
it simply did its work.

Day 118 – People around me changed.
They smiled more,
softened
as if touched by invisible light.

Day 120 – I no longer felt boundaries between self and space.
All things breathed together.
All light knew.

Day 121 – I understood:
There is no "practice"
only Life practicing itself.

"I am no longer cultivating Qi
Qi is cultivating me."

Closing the Appendix – Return to the Living Source

121 days
not time
but a journey to Life's center.

There is no conclusion
for each new day begins as Day One.

There is no "me" from yesterday
only Root Qi living again through every cell today.

ACKNOWLEDGMENTS

Some journeys cannot be measured by time
because each breath, each pulse, each moment of presence is its own teaching.

I do not know whom to thank first
for everyone who crossed my life left behind a light
whether gentle or intense.

I thank my family, where I learned that real love needs no words.

Thank you to friends, colleagues, and silent companions
you reflected me by being yourselves.

Thank you for the challenges

because of you, I no longer believe in strength,
but began to trust Life.

Thank you to the readers
those quietly walking their own path
for if you're holding this book,
it means the Root Qi has called you.

And above all,
I bow in gratitude to Life
the invisible and most patient teacher
who showed me how to see, how to release,
and how to live without searching.

"When Qi returns to Marrow, Marrow gives rise to Clarity,
When Clarity becomes Light -Mind gives rise to Virtue,
When Virtue transforms Matter- the Way flows on its own."

With deep gratitude to all forms of life
for in every encounter,
Life is teaching us what we most need to see.

— Hồ Quang Bình
The Peace Scholar

ABOUT THE AUTHOR

Hồ Quang Bình is the founder of the Ontological Code (Code Bản Thể) – Root Qi,
a system of living knowledge that draws from traditional Qi studies, insight from modern neuroscience, and bioenergetic embodiment.

He does not write to teach
but to record the journey of life realizing itself through
body – qi– mind– wisdom and light

Across 1,700+ essays on Code Bản Thể Journal,
he shares first-hand revelations of Root Qi
where breath becomes knowledge,
the body becomes a sacred tool,
and life becomes the true teacher.

"Code Bản Thể – The Root of Living Light"
distills 121 days of inner practice during which
body, Qi, mind, and knowing unified into the Ontological Radiation Field
a state where life flows on its own, beyond effort.

"No one awakens anyone.
Only Life awakens itself through human form."

COPYRIGHT INFORMATION

CLOSING REFLECTION

If you are reading these final lines
know that the energy of Life is flowing through you.

You did not find this book
Root Qi found you.

Live slowly.
Breathe deeply.
Let Life breathe through you.

"Root Qi is not a philosophy
but the peaceful return of every cell."

— Hồ Quang Bình
The Peace Scholar

www.ingramcontent.com/pod-product-compliance
Lightning Source LLC
LaVergne TN
LVHW090433210926
848480LV00002B/804